SECRETS OF TRUE HAPPINESS

by

Tai Sheridan, Ph.D.

Secrets of True Happiness

ISBN-13: 978-1475013542
ISBN-10: 147501354X

© 2012 Tai Sheridan

Website: www.taisheridan.com

Email: tai@taishcridan.com

BOOKS BY TAI SHERIDAN

Buddha in Blue Jeans Series

Buddha in Blue Jeans: An Extremely Short Zen Guide to Being Buddha

Relax...You're Going to Die

Secrets of True Happiness

Buddhist Classics in Modern Verse

Celestial Music: Sutras of Emptiness
The Lotus / Diamond / Heart-Wisdom / Loving Kindness Sutras

The Bare Bones Dhammapada: Big Mind Big Love
Buddha's Essential Teachings

The Buddhacarita: A Modern Sequel
The Poetic Saga of Buddha's Life From Birth to Enlightenment

The Zen Wheel of Life Mantra: A Song of Luminous Wisdom and Love / *Based on the Bhavacakra - The Wheel of Life Mandala*

Zen Classics in Modern Verse

The Light of the Ancient Buddhas: Ballads of Emptiness and Awakening / *Based on Keizan's Transmission of the Light*

Rice Eyes: Enlightenment in Dogen's Kitchen
A poetic version of Dogen's Tenzo Kyokun on enlightened living and practice

Snow Falling in Moonlight: Odes in Praise of Dogen's Shobogenzo
Twelve Poems based on Dogen's Shobogenzo:The Treasury of the True Dharma Eye

Warm Zen Practice: A Poetic Version of Dogen's
Bendowa - *The Whole Hearted Way*

Collections and Other Spiritual Books

Buddha's Light Body: Collected Works of Tai Sheridan

Patanjali – Yoga Sutras in Lingo: *The Liberation of Spirit in Modern Metaphors*

DEDICATION

To the man in the moon who is Truly Happy.

Poetry and Hums aren't things which you get,
they're things which get you.
And all you can do is go where they can find you.

- Winnie the Pooh

Contents

Introduction

This is an extremely short, simple, and straight forward book.

It is a universal guide to True Happiness. In my book *Buddha in Blue Jeans*, I encourage sitting quietly. In *The Secrets of Happiness*, I encourage wise living as a way to True Happiness.

When you are truly happy you can be at ease in the world as a Buddha in Blue Jeans: a person of presence, openness, love, and benefit.

Wishing you true happiness,

Tai Sheridan
Kentfield, California 2012

TRUE HAPPINESS

True Happiness is inside of you.

You may look
outside of yourself
for many reasons.
It is a fruitless search
in the wrong place.

True happiness finds you
when you become
content with life
quiet and spacious inside
accepting of whatever
comes your way
and lovingly connected
to the whole universe.

True Happiness
is the result of wise living.

May you be truly happy!

WANTING

You want things
which is natural.

However
if you want
True Happiness
wanting can't run you.

It is easy
to get stuck
on the carousel
of wanting.

A good question
to ask yourself is
'What am I chasing after?"

Contentment with what
you already have
is True Happiness.

May you be truly happy!

ANGER

You get angry.

You get frustrated and hurt.

Feeling angry is human.

Disappointment is always
underneath anger.

Harming yourself
or other people
with your anger
will keep you from
True Happiness.

True Happiness
doesn't hold grudges
or get back.

True happiness
understands forgives
and returns to harmony.

May you be truly happy!

PRIDE

You like feeling
proud of yourself.

Being proud of
who you are
and of your
accomplishments
is natural.

You need
to love yourself
and feel O.K.

If your pride gets
too big though
you stop treasuring
other people and
you stop listening
to the sound
of their lives.

You can't have
True Happiness
if you live
on an island
or if you spend
too much time
in front of
the mirror.

Buddha in Blue Jeans
likes an even
balance sheet.
One for me
one for you
one for me
one for you.

May you be truly happy!

LIFE AND DEATH

You are alive.
This is an
incomprehensible
mystery.

Experiencing aliveness
is more important
than anything you believe.

You can fear it
and worry about it
or you can embrace it.

When being alive
is part of your every moment
True Happiness awakens.

You will die.
This is an
incomprehensible
mystery.

Embracing death
is more important
than anything you believe.

You can fear it
and worry about it
or you can embrace it.

When death is part
of your every moment
True Happiness awakens.

May you be truly happy!

Uncertainty

Being alive is risk.

Safety and security
are temporary.

Maybe you feel anxious
because you feel uncertain.

Maybe your feel depressed
because you feel uncertain.

Spending your life
looking for certainty
is like chasing
your shadow.

Embracing uncertainty
gives you room
to live and breathe.

Uncertainty is a good friend
that keeps you alert and real.

When you delight in uncertainty
you can be Truly Happy.

May you be truly happy!

Change

Change is the way of life.

It throws you
when you forget
it is your best friend.

When you react
to change
as if it isn't
supposed to happen
you have forgotten
what it is to be alive.

The more you fear change
the more you are stuck
on thinking you know
exactly who you are.

Change is the
harbinger of death
because each change
is a death of the old.

Change is also
the birth announcement
of the wondrous new.

Grief is the real response
to the death of the old
and joy is the real response

to the birth of the new.

Experiencing your joy and grief
without being thrown off kilter
is True Happiness.

May you be truly happy!

OPENNESS

Openness means
not being attached
to your own
point of view.

This means
there is no right way
of seeing anything.

Many people have told you
that you are wrong
for how you see things
so it is easy to get
invested in being right.

Your sense of being right
will bring you grief
and will ruin
your relationships.

The only thing
a Truly Happy person can say
is 'this is how I see it!'.

People respond to
an open person
with love.

That's because
openness is love.

May you be truly happy!

TIME

Time is a flowing river
that you can't grab.

When you want to grab it
you have forgotten
that your life
is the flowing river
and that you can
only experience now.

Everything that exists
is an expression of time
because it flows
from not existing
to hanging around
to not existing again.

When you are
anxious about time
you have probably forgotten
to breathe relax let go of control.

If you decide to live
in cosmic time
rather than in
wrist watch time
you will have a
very big perspective.

Your memory
is a distortion of time
because you begin to believe
that the past is still real.

Your wishes
are a distortion of time
because you begin to believe
that the future is real.

Your thoughts about
what is going on now
are a distortion of time
because they keep you
from participating fully
in right now.

When you return to real time
your clock registers zero
and you are Truly Happy.

May you be truly happy!

CREATIVITY

Life is creative.

When you are creative
life flows through you.

Creativity exists
beyond good and bad
two culprits that ruin
natural creativity.

True creativity
is beyond compare.
The less you compare
the more you create
in your own way
which frees you to be
spontaneous joyful alive
and happy with
whatever your make.

Everybody is naturally creative.
When you hear the words
"I can't do that"
please toss them
into the trash and
start making something.

Enjoying creativity
without standards
is True Happiness.

May you be truly happy!

WORK

Work is energy
that is channeled
into an activity.

Life is work.

All work
is beneficial to you
and to others.

You are always working.
It isn't defined
by your gender
job role income.

Your value isn't
because of your work.
It is because you are you.

Sometimes you will like
the work you do
sometimes you won't.
Sometimes it is altruistic
sometimes it is just
getting the job done.

If you participate
in your work
without griping
and if you stay connected

to your joyful existence
you can be Truly Happy.

Your resistance to work
is your resistance
to being alive.

There is no retirement
there is only death.

When you define work
as a way of experiencing
total aliveness
your 'work life' becomes
True Happiness.

May you be truly happy!

FAMILY

You belong to family
even if you are
lonely and isolated
which sadly is
the big disease
of modern society.

You need your family
and your family needs you.

Even though families
change shape through
birth death separation
you still belong
completely

When you accept
all that has happened
in your family experience
the good the bad the ugly
you can be Truly Happy.
It is how you got
to where you are today
which is wonderful.

The big True Family
includes everyone
and all things.

Realizing that
the big True Family is you
and that you are the big True Family
is True Happiness.

May you be truly happy!

SOLITUDE

You live within yourself
but are never alone.

Being your own best friend
means enjoying being
with yourself in solitude.

You may avoid solitude
or feel that you don't
have enough time
to be with yourself.

There is always time for solitude
which doesn't punch a clock.
I hope you sit quietly a lot.

Solitude is where
you care for your inner life
and the places that make you
who you are.

It is where you know and
resolve things.

Solitude is where
you make peace with living and dying.

Solitude is where
you are honest with yourself.

When you participate in solitude regularly
you can be Truly Happy.

May you be truly happy!

NATURE

Nature is life.

Spending time close
to nature is celebrating
the wonder of existence.

Nature is not something
that can be conquered
or completely understood.
It will always be a mystery.

You were
conceived by parents
but nature is
the ultimate source
of your existence.

Being in love with nature
is True Happiness.

May you be truly happy!

LOVE

Big love is indiscriminate.

It doesn't depend
on a person or an object.

You are Big Love.

Big Love loves
everything equally.

Big Love
is the warp and woof
of existence.

Big Love
is True Happiness.

May you be truly happy!

Buddha in Blue Jeans
is Truly Happy

Buddha in Blue Jeans™

Buddha in Blue Jeans
has a transparent body from being open.

Buddha in Blue Jeans
has big arms from embracing the world.

Buddha in Blue Jeans
has big feet from living a stable life.

Buddha in Blue Jeans
has an open belly from living a balanced life.

Buddha in Blue Jeans

has a warm heart from loving indiscriminately.

Buddha in Blue Jeans
has bright eyes from seeing clearly.

Buddha in Blue Jeans
has a big smile from being Truly Happy.

May you be truly happy!

A WISH FOR THE WORLD

May All Beings Be Happy!

May all Beings Be One!

May All Beings Be Peaceful!

About the Author

Tai Sheridan is a poet, philosopher, and Zen priest with forty years of training in the Shunryu Suzuki lineage. He transforms ancient Buddhist and Zen texts into accessible and inspirational verses. His *Buddha in Blue Jeans* series offers a contemporary approach to Buddhist philosophy and awakening.

Please visit www.taisheridan.com to review, purchase, or download other books and podcasts by this author.

You can contact the author at tai@taisheridan.com

Made in the USA
Lexington, KY
13 January 2013